KU-433-231

VICTORIAN COTTAGES
ADDRESS BOOK

· PARRAGON ·

VICTORIAN COTTAGES

First published in 1996 by Parragon Book Service Ltd
Unit 13-17, Avonbridge Trading Estate
Atlantic Road, Avonmouth
Bristol BS11 9QD
England

Copyright © Parragon Book Service Ltd 1996

ISBN 0-7525-1892-5

Printed in Italy

Produced by Kingfisher Design, London
Art Director: Pedro Prá-Lopez

This address book is sold subject to the condition that it shall not, by way of trade or otherwise,
be lent, resold, hired out or otherwise circulated without the publisher's prior consent
in any form of binding or cover other than that in which it is published
and without similar condition being imposed on the subsequent purchaser.

All information is included by the editors in good faith and is believed to be correct at the time of going to press.
No responsibility can be accepted for error.

Name

Address

Phone   Fax

Name

Address

Phone   Fax

Name

Address

Phone   Fax

Name

Address

Phone   Fax

Name

Address

Phone   Fax

Name

Address

Phone   Fax

Name

Address

Phone   Fax

Name

Address

Phone   Fax

A

Name

Address

Phone   Fax

Name

Address

Phone   Fax

Name

Address

Phone   Fax

Name

Address

Phone   Fax

Name

Address

Phone   Fax

Name

Address

Phone   Fax

Name

Address

Phone   Fax

Name

Address

Phone   Fax

Name

Address

Phone   Fax

Name

Address

Phone   Fax

Name

Address

Phone   Fax

Name

Address

Phone   Fax

Name

Address

Phone   Fax

Name

Address

Phone   Fax

Name

Address

Phone   Fax

Name

Address

Phone   Fax

C

Name

Address

Phone   Fax

Name

Address

Phone   Fax

Name

Address

Phone   Fax

Name

Address

Phone   Fax

Name

Address

Phone   Fax

Name

Address

Phone   Fax

Name

Address

Phone   Fax

Name

Address

Phone   Fax

Name

Address

Phone   Fax

Name

Address

Phone   Fax

Name

Address

Phone   Fax

Name

Address

Phone   Fax

Name

Address

Phone   Fax

Name

Address

Phone   Fax

Name

Address

Phone   Fax

Name

Address

Phone   Fax

D

Name

Address

Phone   Fax

Name

Address

Phone   Fax

Name

Address

Phone   Fax

Name

Address

Phone   Fax

Name

Address

Phone   Fax

Name

Address

Phone   Fax

Name

Address

Phone   Fax

Name

Address

Phone   Fax

Name

Address

Phone   Fax

Name

Address

Phone   Fax

Name

Address

Phone   Fax

Name

Address

Phone   Fax

Name

Address

Phone   Fax

Name

Address

Phone   Fax

Name

Address

Phone   Fax

Name

Address

Phone   Fax

E

Name

Address

Phone   Fax

Name

Address

Phone   Fax

Name

Address

Phone   Fax

Name

Address

Phone   Fax

Name

Address

Phone   Fax

Name

Address

Phone   Fax

Name

Address

Phone   Fax

Name

Address

Phone   Fax

The Cottage by the River, Benjamin William Leader (1831-1923)

E

Name	Name
Address	Address
Phone Fax	Phone Fax
Name	Name
Address	Address
Phone Fax	Phone Fax
Name	Name
Address	Address
Phone Fax	Phone Fax
Name	Name
Address	Address
Phone Fax	Phone Fax

Name

Address

Phone   Fax

Name

Address

Phone   Fax

Name

Address

Phone   Fax

Name

Address

Phone   Fax

Name

Address

Phone   Fax

Name

Address

Phone   Fax

Name

Address

Phone   Fax

Name

Address

Phone   Fax

F

Name

Address

Phone   Fax

Name

Address

Phone   Fax

Name

Address

Phone   Fax

Name

Address

Phone   Fax

Name

Address

Phone   Fax

Name

Address

Phone   Fax

Name

Address

Phone   Fax

Name

Address

Phone   Fax

Family Worship, from the Pears Annual, 1911, Joseph Clark (1834-1926)

G

Name

Address

Phone   Fax

Name

Address

Phone   Fax

Name

Address

Phone   Fax

Name

Address

Phone   Fax

Name

Address

Phone   Fax

Name

Address

Phone   Fax

Name

Address

Phone   Fax

Name

Address

Phone   Fax

Name

Address

Phone   Fax

Name

Address

Phone   Fax

Name

Address

Phone   Fax

Name

Address

Phone   Fax

Name

Address

Phone   Fax

Name

Address

Phone   Fax

Name

Address

Phone   Fax

Name

Address

Phone   Fax

H

Name

Address

Phone   Fax

Name

Address

Phone   Fax

Name

Address

Phone   Fax

Name

Address

Phone   Fax

Name

Address

Phone   Fax

Name

Address

Phone   Fax

Name

Address

Phone   Fax

Name

Address

Phone   Fax

Name

Address

Phone   Fax

Name

Address

Phone   Fax

Name

Address

Phone   Fax

Name

Address

Phone   Fax

Name

Address

Phone   Fax

Name

Address

Phone   Fax

Name

Address

Phone   Fax

Name

Address

Phone   Fax

I

Name

Address

Phone   Fax

Name

Address

Phone   Fax

Name

Address

Phone   Fax

Name

Address

Phone   Fax

Name

Address

Phone   Fax

Name

Address

Phone   Fax

Name

Address

Phone   Fax

Name

Address

Phone   Fax

Name

Address

Phone   Fax

Name

Address

Phone   Fax

Name

Address

Phone   Fax

Name

Address

Phone   Fax

Name

Address

Phone   Fax

Name

Address

Phone   Fax

Name

Address

Phone   Fax

Name

Address

Phone   Fax

J

Name	Name
Address	Address
Phone Fax	Phone Fax
Name	Name
Address	Address
Phone Fax	Phone Fax
Name	Name
Address	Address
Phone Fax	Phone Fax
Name	Name
Address	Address
Phone Fax	Phone Fax

Scammel's Farm (near Peaslake, Surrey), Edward Wilkins Waite (1854-1924)

J

Name

Address

Phone   Fax

Name

Address

Phone   Fax

Name

Address

Phone   Fax

Name

Address

Phone   Fax

Name

Address

Phone   Fax

Name

Address

Phone   Fax

Name

Address

Phone   Fax

Name

Address

Phone   Fax

Name

Address

Phone   Fax

Name

Address

Phone   Fax

Name

Address

Phone   Fax

Name

Address

Phone   Fax

Name

Address

Phone   Fax

Name

Address

Phone   Fax

Name

Address

Phone   Fax

Name

Address

Phone   Fax

K

Name

Address

Phone   Fax

Name

Address

Phone   Fax

Name

Address

Phone   Fax

Name

Address

Phone   Fax

Name

Address

Phone   Fax

Name

Address

Phone   Fax

Name

Address

Phone   Fax

Name

Address

Phone   Fax

Ballaugh, Isle of Man, Henry John Yeend King (1855-1924)

L

Name

Address

Phone   Fax

Name

Address

Phone   Fax

Name

Address

Phone   Fax

Name

Address

Phone   Fax

Name

Address

Phone   Fax

Name

Address

Phone   Fax

Name

Address

Phone   Fax

Name

Address

Phone   Fax

Name

Address

Phone   Fax

Name

Address

Phone   Fax

Name

Address

Phone   Fax

Name

Address

Phone   Fax

Name

Address

Phone   Fax

Name

Address

Phone   Fax

Name

Address

Phone   Fax

Name

Address

Phone   Fax

M

Name

Address

Phone   Fax

Name

Address

Phone   Fax

Name

Address

Phone   Fax

Name

Address

Phone   Fax

Name

Address

Phone   Fax

Name

Address

Phone   Fax

Name

Address

Phone   Fax

Name

Address

Phone   Fax

M

Name

Address

Phone   Fax

Name

Address

Phone   Fax

Name

Address

Phone   Fax

Name

Address

Phone   Fax

Name

Address

Phone   Fax

Name

Address

Phone   Fax

Name

Address

Phone   Fax

Name

Address

Phone   Fax

N

Name

Address

Phone   Fax

Name

Address

Phone   Fax

Name

Address

Phone   Fax

Name

Address

Phone   Fax

Name

Address

Phone   Fax

Name

Address

Phone   Fax

Name

Address

Phone   Fax

Name

Address

Phone   Fax

Name

Address

Phone   Fax

Name

Address

Phone   Fax

Name

Address

Phone   Fax

Name

Address

Phone   Fax

Name

Address

Phone   Fax

Name

Address

Phone   Fax

Name

Address

Phone   Fax

Name

Address

Phone   Fax

O

Name

Address

Phone   Fax

Name

Address

Phone   Fax

Name

Address

Phone   Fax

Name

Address

Phone   Fax

Name

Address

Phone   Fax

Name

Address

Phone   Fax

Name

Address

Phone   Fax

Name

Address

Phone   Fax

Country Scene, Louis Robert Carrier-Belleuse (1848-1913)

O

Name

Address

Phone   Fax

Name

Address

Phone   Fax

Name

Address

Phone   Fax

Name

Address

Phone   Fax

Name

Address

Phone   Fax

Name

Address

Phone   Fax

Name

Address

Phone   Fax

Name

Address

Phone   Fax

Name

Address

Phone   Fax

Name

Address

Phone   Fax

Name

Address

Phone   Fax

Name

Address

Phone   Fax

Name

Address

Phone   Fax

Name

Address

Phone   Fax

Name

Address

Phone   Fax

Name

Address

Phone   Fax

P

Name

Address

Phone   Fax

Name

Address

Phone   Fax

Name

Address

Phone   Fax

Name

Address

Phone   Fax

Name

Address

Phone   Fax

Name

Address

Phone   Fax

Name

Address

Phone   Fax

Name

Address

Phone   Fax

Name

Address

Phone   Fax

Name

Address

Phone   Fax

Name

Address

Phone   Fax

Name

Address

Phone   Fax

Name

Address

Phone   Fax

Name

Address

Phone   Fax

Name

Address

Phone   Fax

Name

Address

Phone   Fax

Name	Name
Address	Address
Phone Fax	Phone Fax
Name	Name
Address	Address
Phone Fax	Phone Fax
Name	Name
Address	Address
Phone Fax	Phone Fax
Name	Name
Address	Address
Phone Fax	Phone Fax

Name

Address

Phone   Fax

Name

Address

Phone   Fax

Name

Address

Phone   Fax

Name

Address

Phone   Fax

Name

Address

Phone   Fax

Name

Address

Phone   Fax

Name

Address

Phone   Fax

Name

Address

Phone   Fax

R

Name

Address

Phone   Fax

Name

Address

Phone   Fax

Name

Address

Phone   Fax

Name

Address

Phone   Fax

Name

Address

Phone   Fax

Name

Address

Phone   Fax

Name

Address

Phone   Fax

Name

Address

Phone   Fax

R

Figures with Donkeys outside a Cottage, William Shayer Snr (1788-1879)

S

Name

Address

Phone   Fax

Name

Address

Phone   Fax

Name

Address

Phone   Fax

Name

Address

Phone   Fax

Name

Address

Phone   Fax

Name

Address

Phone   Fax

Name

Address

Phone   Fax

Name

Address

Phone   Fax

Name

Address

Phone   Fax

Name

Address

Phone   Fax

Name

Address

Phone   Fax

Name

Address

Phone   Fax

Name

Address

Phone   Fax

Name

Address

Phone   Fax

Name

Address

Phone   Fax

Name

Address

Phone   Fax

T

Name

Address

Phone   Fax

Name

Address

Phone   Fax

Name

Address

Phone   Fax

Name

Address

Phone   Fax

Name

Address

Phone   Fax

Name

Address

Phone   Fax

Name

Address

Phone   Fax

Name

Address

Phone   Fax

Village of Bowness, Cumberland, James Burrell-Smith (active 1824-1897)

T

Name

Address

Phone   Fax

Name

Address

Phone   Fax

Name

Address

Phone   Fax

Name

Address

Phone   Fax

Name

Address

Phone   Fax

Name

Address

Phone   Fax

Name

Address

Phone   Fax

Name

Address

Phone   Fax

Name

Address

Phone   Fax

Name

Address

Phone   Fax

Name

Address

Phone   Fax

Name

Address

Phone   Fax

Name

Address

Phone   Fax

Name

Address

Phone   Fax

Name

Address

Phone   Fax

Name

Address

Phone   Fax

UV

Name

Address

Phone   Fax

Name

Address

Phone   Fax

Name

Address

Phone   Fax

Name

Address

Phone   Fax

Name

Address

Phone   Fax

Name

Address

Phone   Fax

Name

Address

Phone   Fax

Name

Address

Phone   Fax

UV

Padworth Mill on the River Kennet, Edward Wilkins Waite (1854-1924)

W

Name

Address

Phone   Fax

Name

Address

Phone   Fax

Name

Address

Phone   Fax

Name

Address

Phone   Fax

Name

Address

Phone   Fax

Name

Address

Phone   Fax

Name

Address

Phone   Fax

Name

Address

Phone   Fax

W

Name

Address

Phone   Fax

Name

Address

Phone   Fax

Name

Address

Phone   Fax

Name

Address

Phone   Fax

Name

Address

Phone   Fax

Name

Address

Phone   Fax

Name

Address

Phone   Fax

Name

Address

Phone   Fax

X Y Z

Name

Address

Phone   Fax

Name

Address

Phone   Fax

Name

Address

Phone   Fax

Name

Address

Phone   Fax

Name

Address

Phone   Fax

Name

Address

Phone   Fax

Name

Address

Phone   Fax

Name

Address

Phone   Fax

Old Cottage, Colwyn Bay, Isaac Cooke (1846-1922)

X Y Z

Name

Address

Phone   Fax

Name

Address

Phone   Fax

Name

Address

Phone   Fax

Name

Address

Phone   Fax

Name

Address

Phone   Fax

Name

Address

Phone   Fax

Name

Address

Phone   Fax

Name

Address

Phone   Fax

ACKNOWLEDGEMENTS

The publishers would like to thank the following for their kind permission
to reproduce the paintings in this address book:

Bridgeman Art Library, London:
Bonhams, London;
Christie's, London;
A & F Pears Ltd, London;
Ackermann and Johnson Ltd, London;
Gavin Graham Gallery, London;
Victoria & Albert Museum, London;
King Street Galleries, London;
Private Collections.